Good Old Tunes

Traditional

FOLK HARP

Music of Beauty and Grace

advancing beginner to intermediate

arranged by Susan Call Hutchison

Foreword

Arranged on my Harpsicle® 26-string harp, this collection of soothing and familiar music was designed so that even with a smaller harp with no levers (C-tuning) you can achieve a graceful, professional sound.

Many of these arrangements can be played on even smaller harps, - like the 19 string Fireside and the Waring kit harps - by shifting the music one octave higher. And you will find music to play even on lap harps and hand-held harps. I hope you love learning and playing these pieces as much as I enjoyed arranging them for you!

Contents

Introduction

For thousands of years, harps - remarkably similar in design to your folk harp - have been lifting spirits, soothing suffering, and bringing comfort to the weary.

It was a fun challenge to find restful music that could be played on a relatively small, unlevered harp in C-tuning – and then to arrange it with no accidentals, while keeping the harmonies professional and interesting. I am pleased with the result, and I offer it to you with hopes that you will appreciate the music and be proud to play it for your listeners.

I wanted this to be an accessible book – suiting the needs of beginners who are just starting to play melody lines as well as players advancing into adding harmony and chords. I wrote it for "26-String" harps (like the Harpsicle®) – but all of the melodies and most of the harmonies can be played on even smaller harps.

BONUS: These arrangements also sound wonderful on piano.

Tips for beginning harp players:

- You can still get a beautiful sound by playing the melody alone.
- The melody is always the top line of notes.
- Once you are familiar with playing the melody, try adding some harmony!
- Sometimes the harmony is written in the top staff, under the melody, and sometimes it is all written in in the bottom staff, to be played with the left hand.
- The left-hand staff will sometimes be bass clef, and sometimes treble clef.
- The songs that use the bass clef for left hand can be played one octave higher.
- Songs with a bass line that goes *below* the lowest note on your harp can be played one octave higher.

Please enjoy and use these tunes to bless yourself and others through your harp journey!

Susan Call Hutchison
Musical Director
Good Old Tunes Publications

Barbara Allen

Old English
Arranged by Susan Call Hutchison

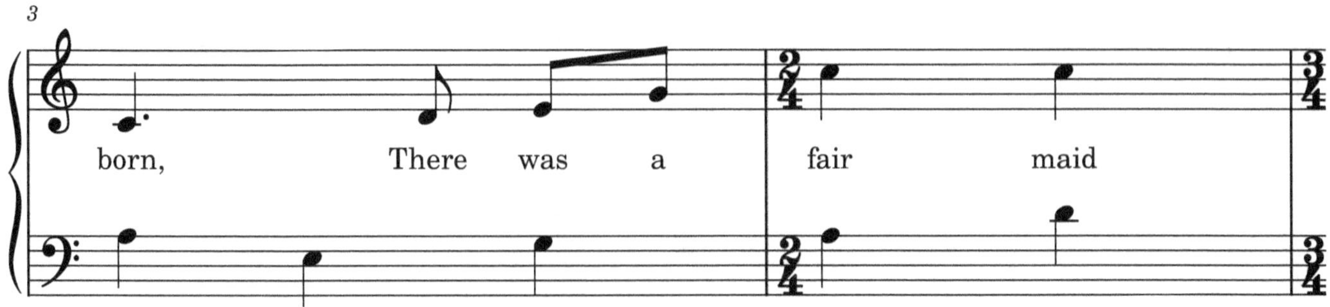

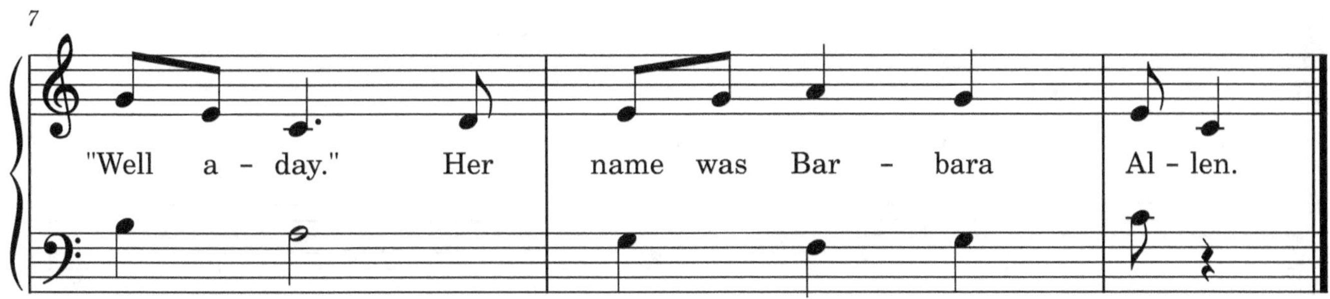

All Through the Night

Sir Harold Boulton

Welsh Air
arranged by Susan Call Hutchison

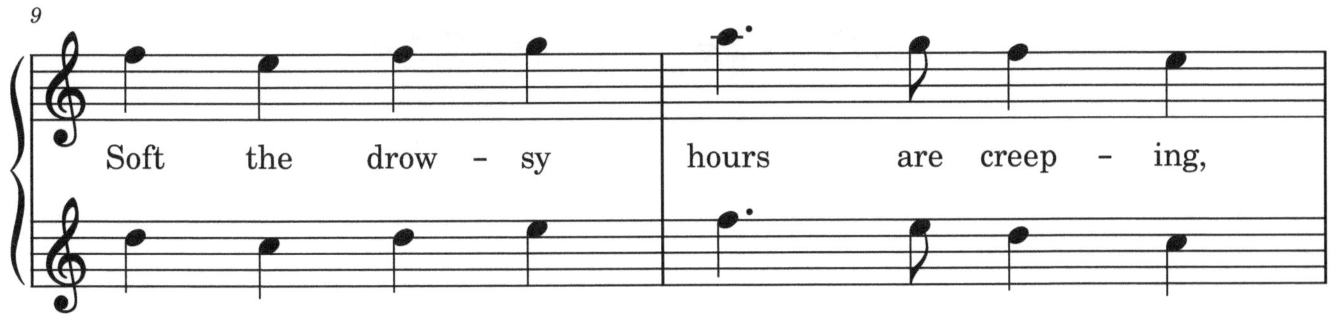

Soft the drow - sy hours are creep - ing,

Hill and vale in slum - ber sleep - ing,

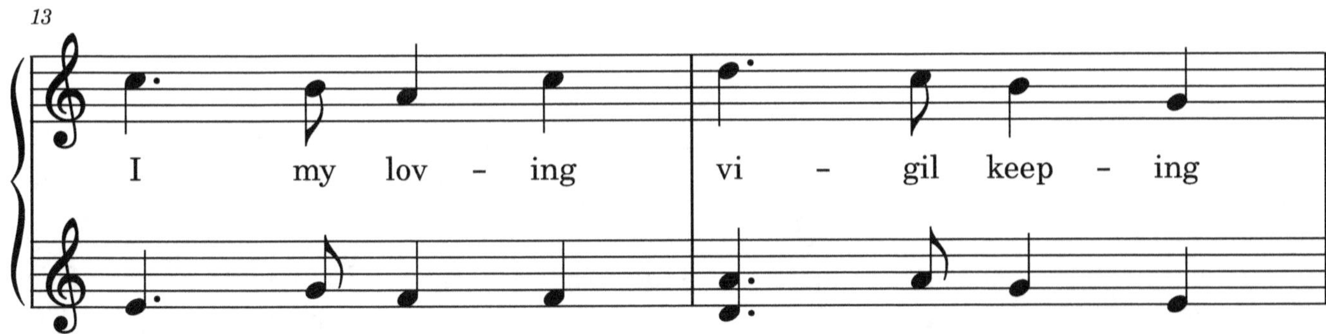

I my lov - ing vi - gil keep - ing

All through the night.

Good Old Tunes

Annie Laurie

William Douglas
and Lady John Scott

Lady John Scott
Arranged by Susan Call Hutchison

Expressively, with freedom of rhythm

7
me her pro - mise true. Gi'ed me her pro - mise
e'er the sun shone on. That e'er the sun shone
voice is low and sweet. Her voice is low and

10
Chorus
true, which ne'er for - got will be. And for
on, And dark blue is her e'e.
sweet, An'she's a' the world to me.

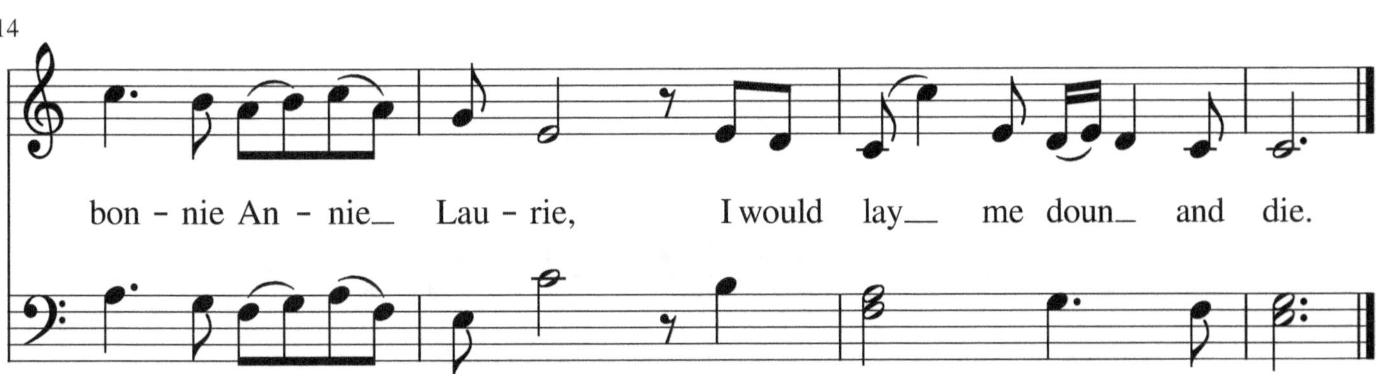
14
bon - nie An - nie_ Lau - rie, I would lay_ me doun_ and die.

Good Old Tunes

The Ash Grove

Thomas Oliphant

Traditional Welsh Tune
arranged by Susan Call Hutchison

Andante

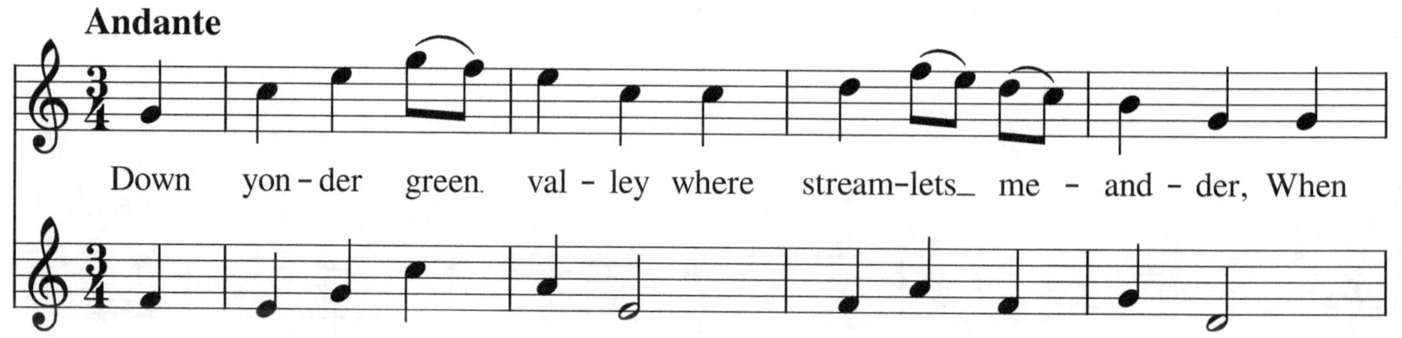

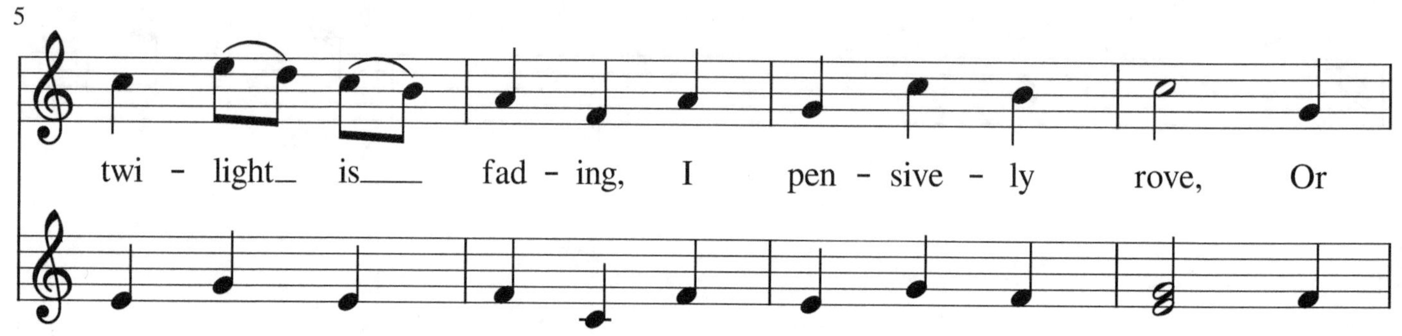

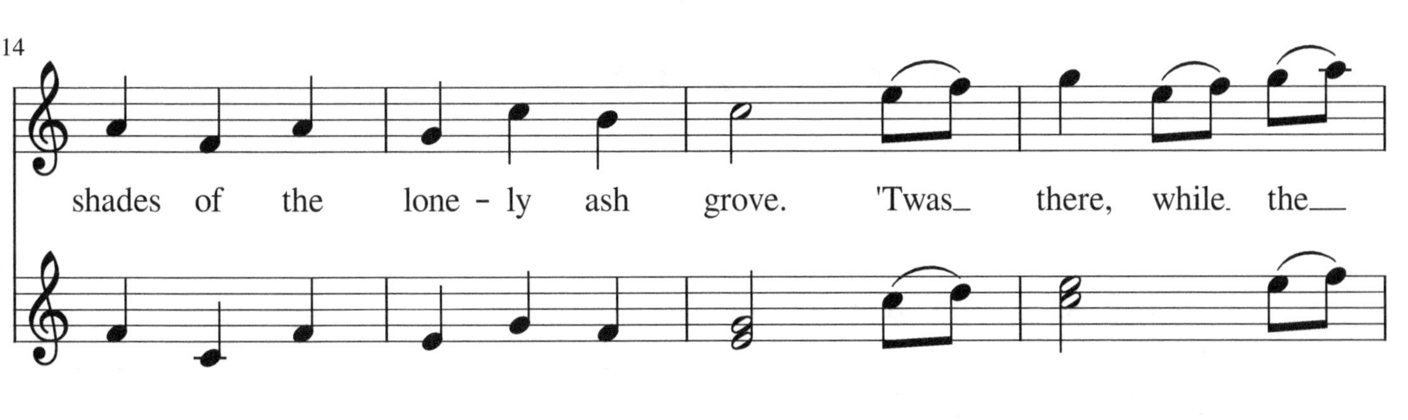
14
shades of the lone - ly ash grove. 'Twas_ there, while. the__

18
black - bird was cheer - ful - ly_ sing - ing, I first met_ my_

22
dear one, the joy of my heart! A - round us for_ glad-ness the

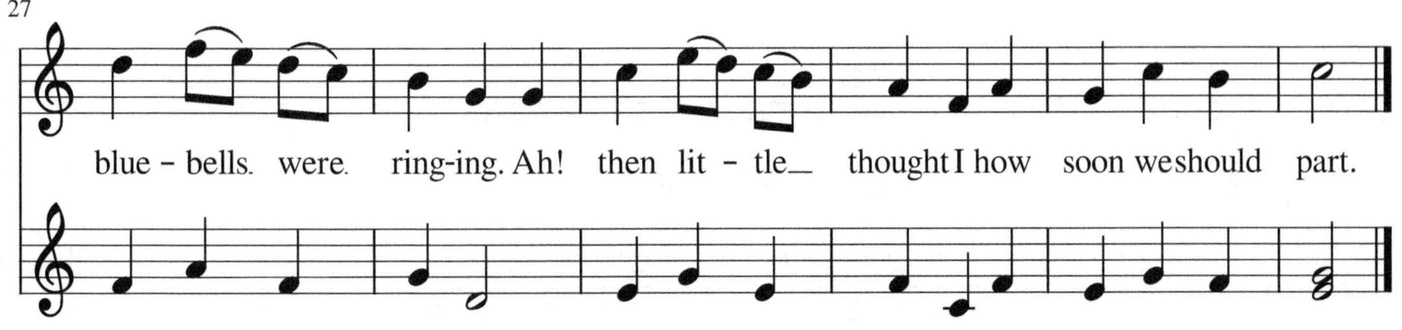
27
blue - bells. were. ring-ing. Ah! then lit - tle_ thought I how soon we should part.

Good Old Tunes

Aura Lea

George R. Poulton
arranged by Susan Call Hutchison

Au - ra Lea! Au - ra Lea!

Maid of gol - den hair!

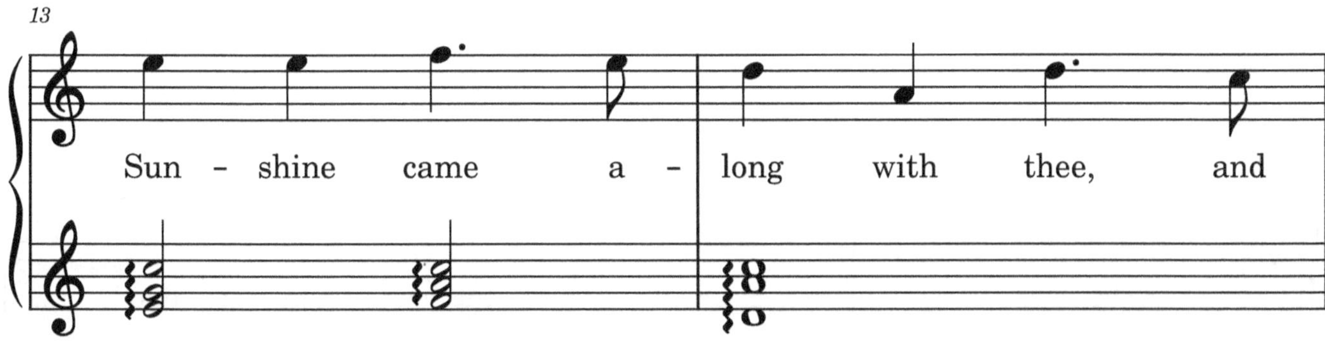
Sun - shine came a - long with thee, and

swal - lows in the air.

Black is the Color of My True Love's Hair

Traditional Scotch Appalatchian
arranged by Susan Call Hutchison

Andante

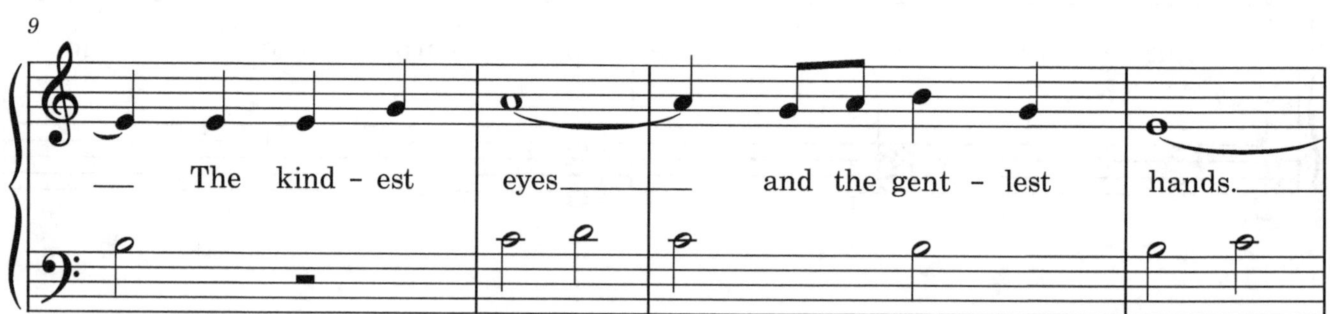

Good Old Tunes

Oh Shenandoah

Traditional
arranged by Susan Call Hutchison

Down in the Valley

Traditional
Arranged by Susan Call Hutchison

As a country waltz

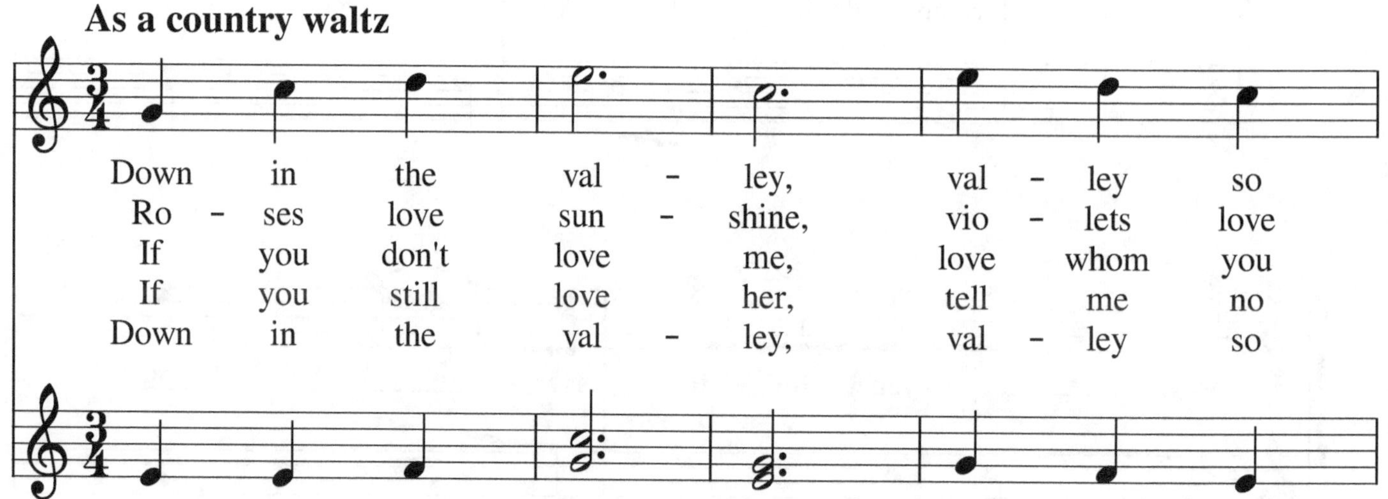

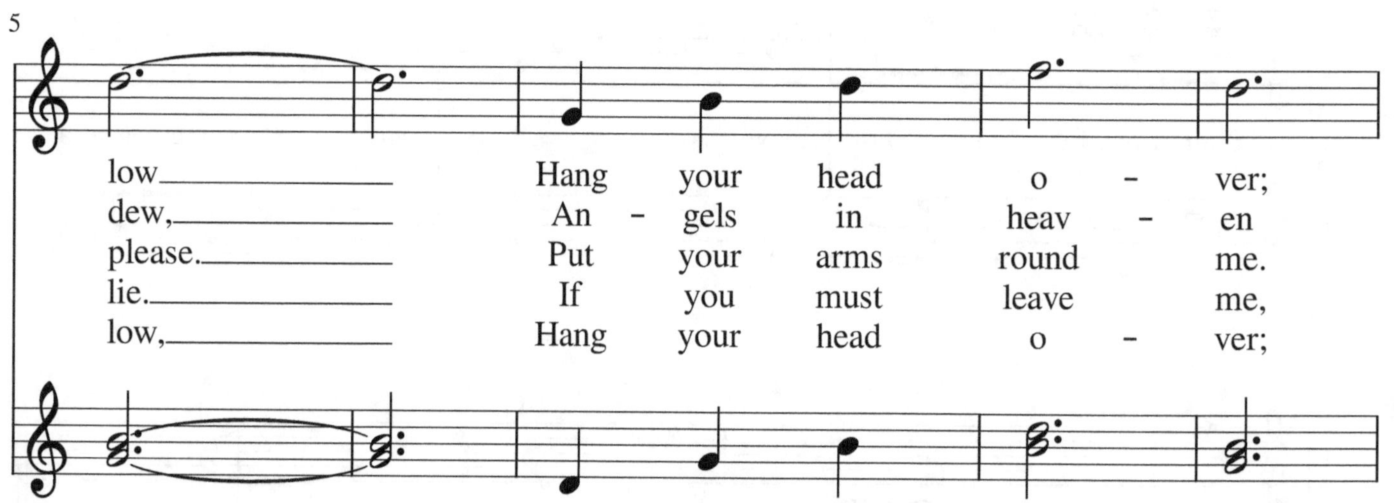

10

hear the wind blow._______ Hear the wind blow,
know I love you._______ Know I love you,
Give my heart ease._______ Give my heart ease,
tell me good - bye._______ Tell me good - bye,
hear the wind blow._______ Hear the wind blow,

15

love, hear the wind blow._______ Hang your head
love, know I love you._______ An - gels in
love, give my heart ease._______ Put your arms
love, tell me good - bye._______ If you must
love, hear the wind blow._______ Hang your head

20

o - ver; hear the wind blow._______________
heav - en know I love you._______________
round me; give my heart ease._______________
leave me, tell me good - bye._______________
ov - er; hear the wind blow._______________

Emperor Waltz

Johann Strauss
arranged by Susan Call Hutchison

Andante

Fine

17
now in strict 3/4 time

21

25

29
D.C. al Fine

Goin' Home

Theme from New World Symphony

Williams Arms Fisher

Anton Dvorak
arranged by Susan Call Hutchison

Slowly and peacefully

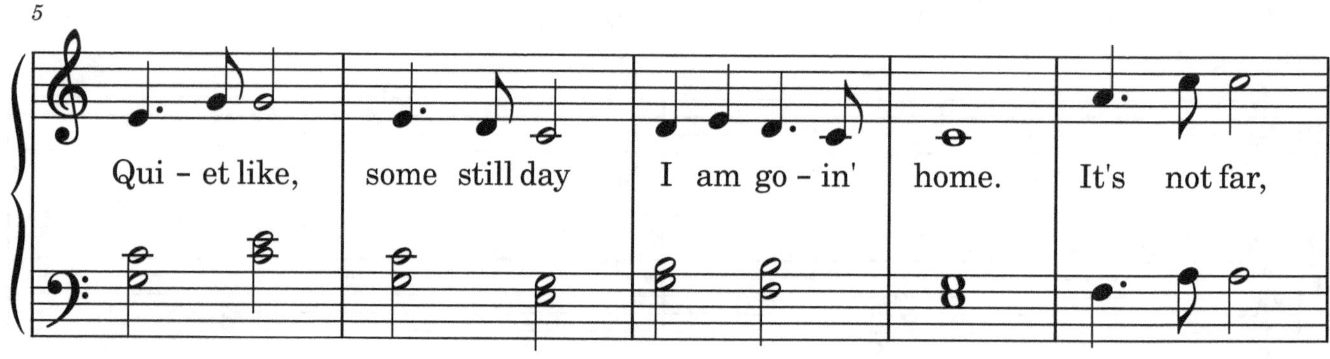

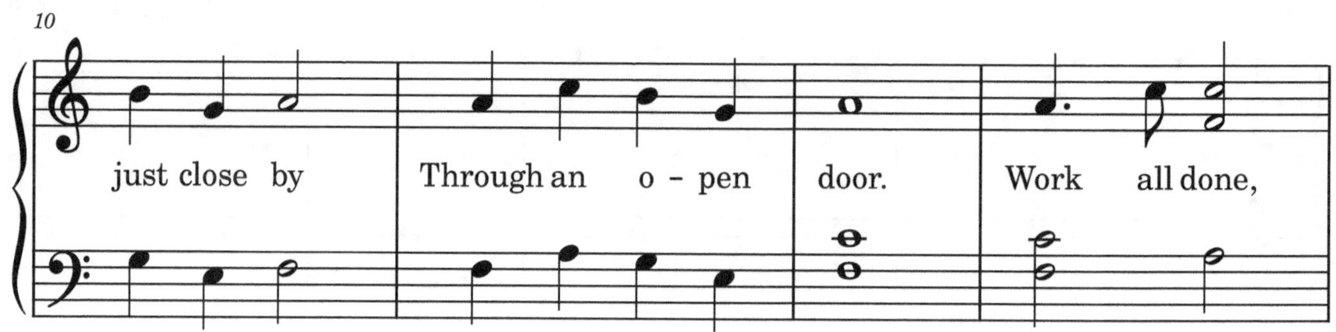

14
care laid by, Nev - er fear no more. Morn - in' star,

18
light the way, Rest - less dream all gone. Shad - ows gone,

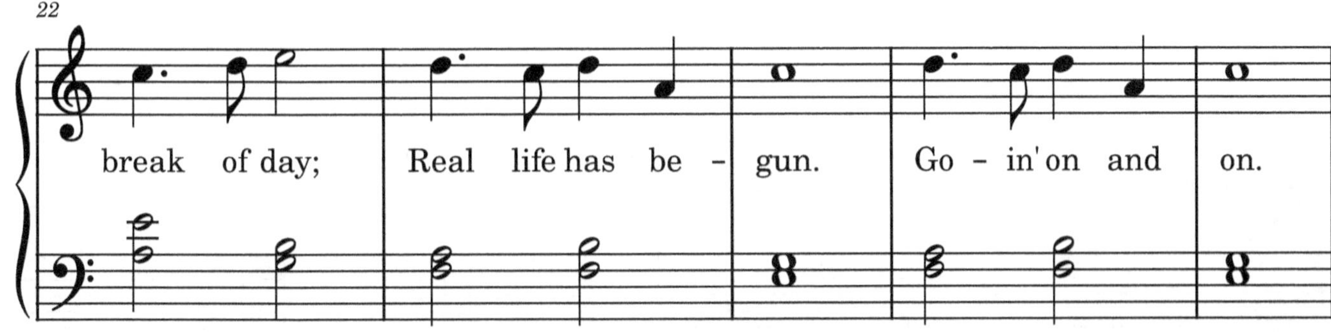
22
break of day; Real life has be - gun. Go - in' on and on.

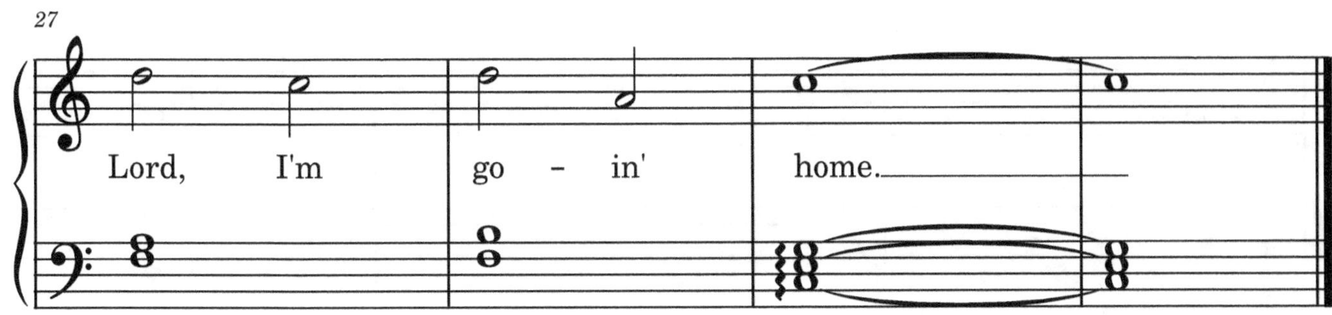
27
Lord, I'm go - in' home.

Good Old Tunes

Greensleeves

Traditional English
arranged by Susan Call Hutchison

Good Old Tunes
Lullaby

Johannes Brahms
arranged by Susan Call Hutchison

Good Old Tunes

The Riddle Song
(I Gave My Love a Cherry)

Traditional Appalachian
arranged by Susan Call Hutchison

Lento

had no end. I gave my love a bab - y with no cry-in'.
has no end? How can there be a bab - y with no cry-ing?
got no end. A bab - y, when it's sleep-ing's got no cry-in'.

Scarborough Fair

Old English Tune
by Susan Call Hutchison

B
20

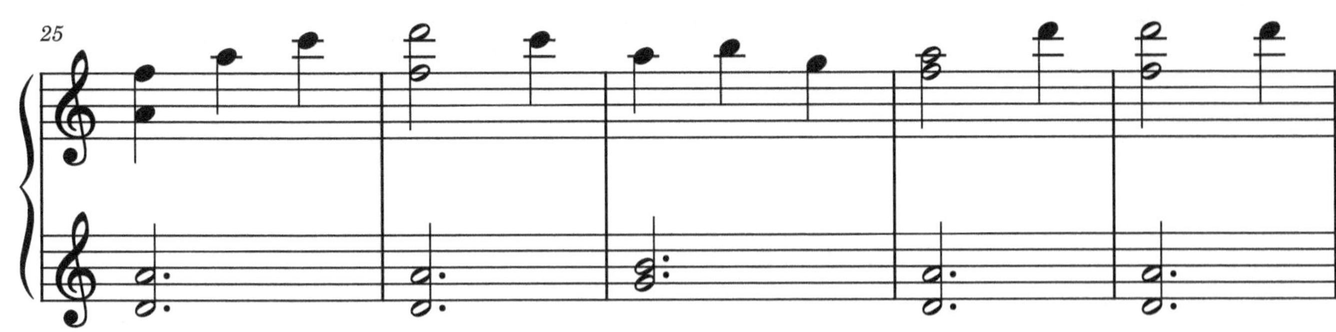

25

30

36
rit.

Good Old Tunes
Simple Gifts

Joseph Brackett, Jr.
arranged by Susan Call Hutchison

Andante

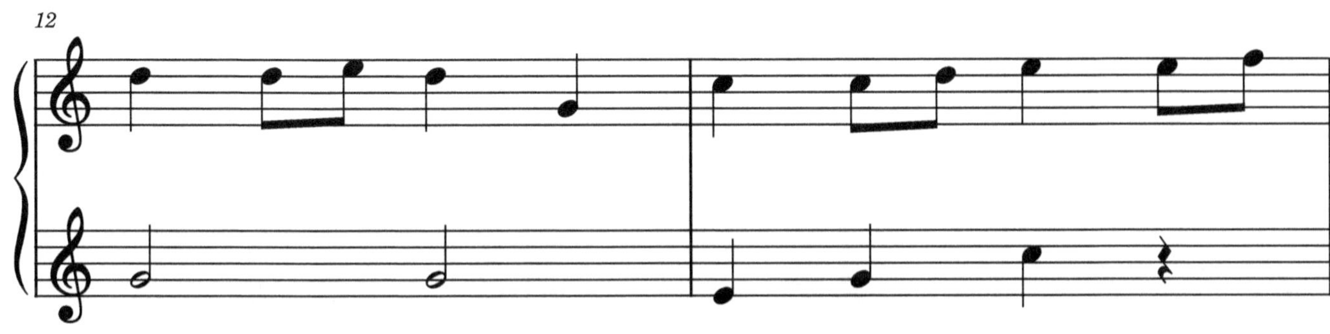

Song Without Words
from Second Suite in F

Gustav Holst
arranged by Susan Call Hutchison

Theme from First Symphony

Johannes Brahms
arranged by Susan Call Hutchison

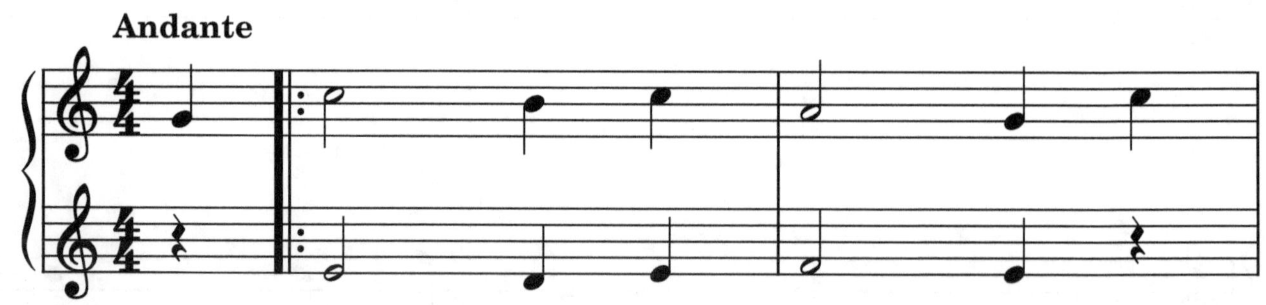

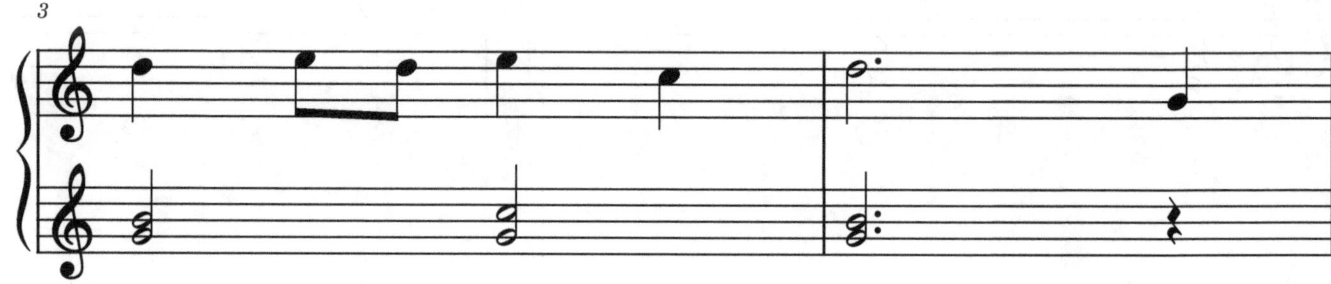

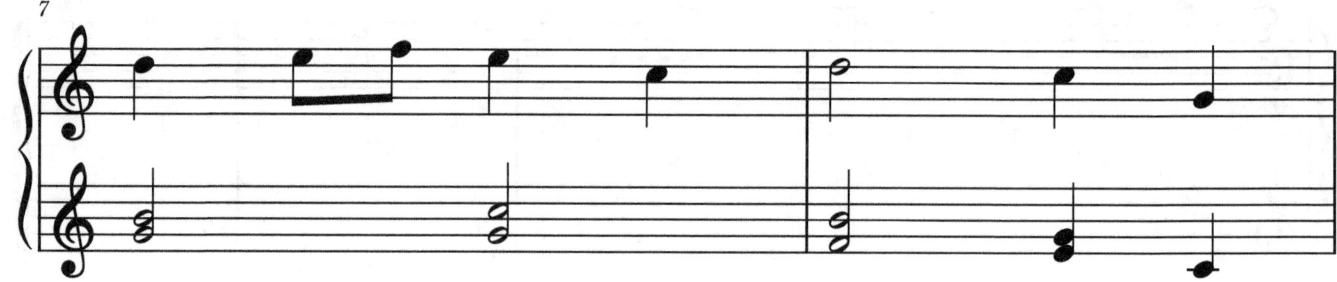

The Water is Wide

Traditional
arranged by Susan Call Hutchison

Adagio

But give me a boat

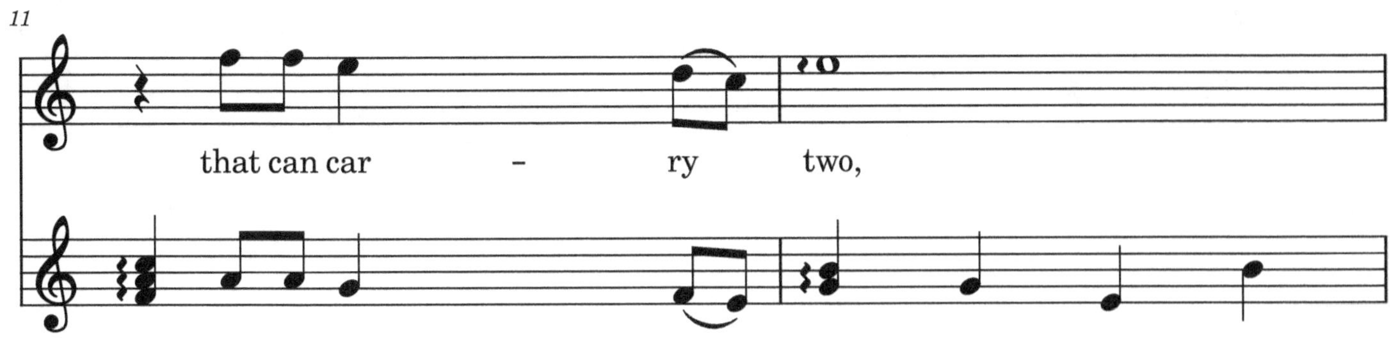
that can car - ry two,

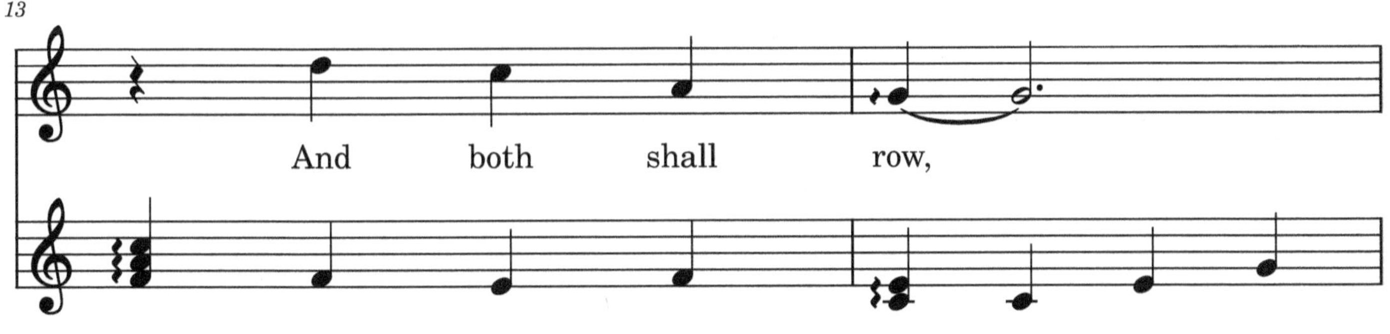
And both shall row,

My love and I.
slowing to the end

Good Old Tunes

Wayfaring Stranger

Traditional
arranged by Susan Call Hutchison

Andante

there_ to meet my moth-er. I know she'll be there when. I__

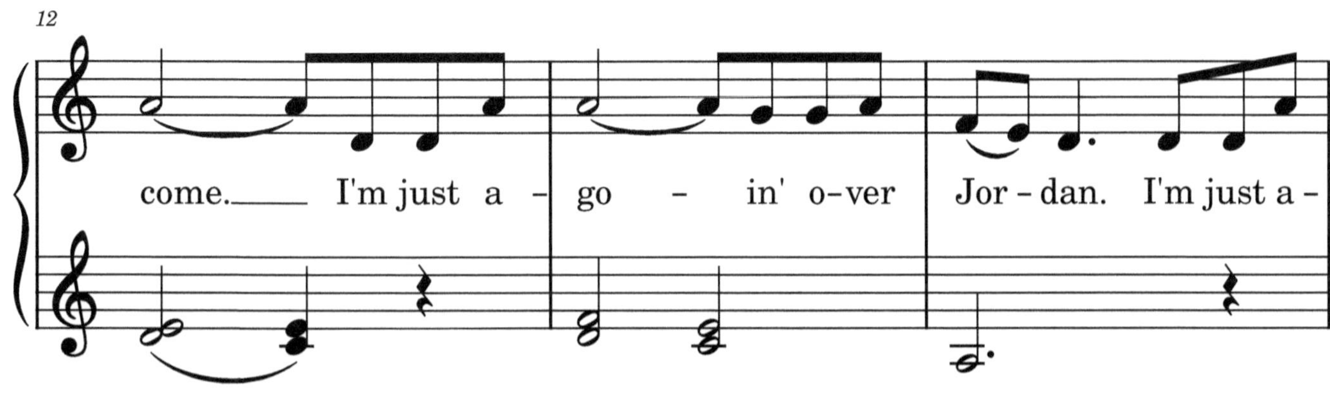
come.___ I'm just a - go - in' o-ver Jor - dan. I'm just a -

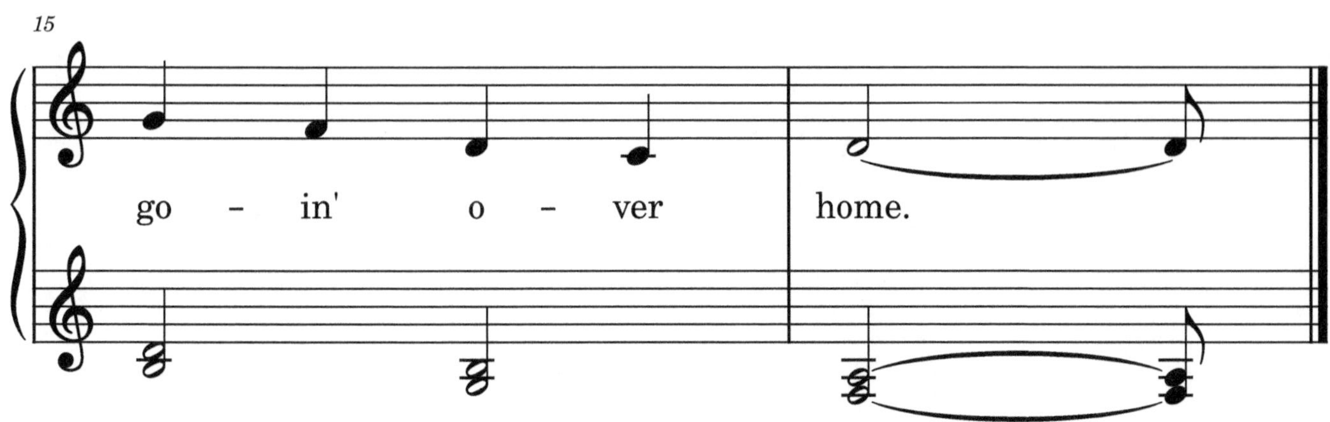
go - in' o - ver home.